MARGARET & DUSTY

Other books by Alice Notley:

165 Meeting House Lane

Phoebe Light

Incidentals in the Day World

Alice Ordered Me to Be Made

For Frank O'Hara's Birthday

A Diamond Necklace

Songs for the Unborn Second Baby

Doctor Williams' Heiresses

When I Was Alive

Waltzing Matilda

How Spring Comes

Sorrento

Poems by Alice Notley

Margaret & Dusty

Coffee House Press :: St. Paul :: 1985

Cover photograph by Rochelle Kraut

Some of these poems have appeared in the following magazines: *Ink, Oink, The World, Ahnoi, Lips, Little Light,* & *Tangerine.* The poem "Morning Comb" was printed on a postcard by The Alternative Press. The author would also like to thank Simon Pettet for his help in the preparation of this manuscript.

The publishers wish to thank the National Endowment for the Arts, a federal agency, for a Small Press Assistance Grant that aided in the production of this book.

Published by Coffee House Press. First printing.

Coffee House Press books are available to the trade from Bookpeople, Bookslinger, Publishers Group West, Inland Book Company, and Small Press Distribution.

Library of Congress Cataloging in Publication Data

Notley, Alice, 1945–
    Margaret & Dusty.

    I. Title.   II. Title: Margaret and Dusty.
PS3564.079M3 1985   811'.54   84-27472
ISBN 0-918273-08-0 (pbk.)

To Anselm & Edmund

TABLE OF CONTENTS

You Now Holding This Book in Hand

The man kissed her hand. Little earrings. They're about
to kiss mouths. She talks into a microphone. All these
men in caps & jackets come into the room. One man is
crying; her hand briefly cups his chin. A man dancing
with a coat is covered by snow. It's snowing. The man &
the woman are inside the coat in the snow. He's behind
the wheel; the boy glares at her long hair. They must
be doctors, & the younger one looks Japanese. There
are ancient bright sails above their boat. An angel in
a cloche. An instant of gold foil. They two have
lined faces so other people with lined faces will know how
to love them. A woman with folded arms & near a
lampshade. The blonde Chinese fade with the dusk. Barbed
wire & tree trunks. Big chair & groceries. A coffeepot
the size of a thousand-year-old man. Two in front of the
Confederate flag. She kisses the man on his cheek.

Morning Comb

Comb out ashes
    & early-morning dew
comb the earth
    but the rain combs itself

comb a shriven woman
comb your love's love
    I've never heard of shriven
comb your ears Alice

comb the Greek archipelago
    November's Child
comb a scrapbook from your youth
    comb a small Dynasty trophy
comb among her papers ca. 1973
    comb your sort of psyche

comb some volcanoes & icebergs
    into the deep —
But the sun combs itself
    scarlet & everywhere

In Ancient December

       in the ideal American
       Willie Nelson, poet laureate
       hapless which one
       his silvery voice floated down
       & pitiless King
       & cold cold Persephone sobbed
       & a dancing carrot

          . . . She told me you were good,
you were gonna do just fine. There's several ways to
use your pants. But only one sure way down. To go to
bed & dream of apartment in flames, rather, small fires,
here & there, & tall & slender at the door? Could I
lead her out without them? Could she leave without
everyone as I never have in any dream ever? I can't
keep my eyes open here. For example if Old Diane as
Eurydice. Who knocked a pervert downstairs when she was
forty; has a blind old boyfriend now whose whore old
girlfriend broke her nose; her son works for the Mafia.
A survivor is a woman who teaches you everything strangely
after some years of knowing, in a sudden and flash you
barely notice, while I'm learning it too listening washing
a dish & wondering why I learn from the one who returned
from her & which of us two will sing a song of it? And
she doesn't even need it. Does she listen to, to
Vic Damone? Maybe. Who's her favorite singer, Ted?
Perry Como, followed closely by Mario Lanza & Frank Sinatra.
Though probably she thinks her son had a beautiful voice
never did nothin with it. Oh God I still can't wake up.
Connie Francis. Get the humor of that? That's Diane. If

I can wake on up:

The song called "Get Away"

Never leave you
Never leave here
Get away by
Telephone, by starpoint by access

Never leave story
Never leave breaking
Get away by chair
By bend
By River mine

Never never leave you
Or kind of thing
Or talking to
It being later now
And never leave you. . . .

Can you worship loss? I can't remember it. I forgot to
sing it off from happening I had to arrange the flowers,
thousands everywhere, & thinly & it being purple I forgot
to see it ten thousand times. She forgot to. She
forgot to too. She would have forgotten anyway. She
didn't forget at any rate, she didn't anything. I didn't
either. I woke up I woke up again & I can't remember I
guess that's just it, but I didn't forget to sing this
time, but I forget what I'm singing. What am I singing?
Singing singing? What am I singing?

Furniture Light

Sun on my cheek, bird
just outside my closed eyes —
shutters and steampipes —
sun dances, curtain
plays.
      Stick-figure girl
come to adore
her again. 1/7/82.

"Just another
lovely old general? Do
you remember Tom
Boerwinkle's stance? Why
are we so happy?"

All my life,

since I was ten,

I've been waiting

to be in

this hell here

with you;

all I've ever

wanted, and

still do:

Macho Daisy Duck

People are only sane when they're writing
This ain't a goddamned Giacometti Plaza you know
People harass their mothers. Go on you violin.
People need money. The rain needs to rain, a little or a lot.
People's foot hurts. From what? I don't know.
There's some clay that's stuck to the bacon bag
My eye doctor was really very funny today.
After four days people find their seersucker pants
Their little shorty shorts & their black brassiere.
People try to locate the trouble with everything.
I am a poor little orphan with only one mother & one father.
There's Camille Pissarro, waiting for the bus.
People 'on't go without, no more I shall
The morning glories are starved into blooming
The man smiles at people with his two gold teeth
I just gave him a bottlecap worth twenty-five cents.
He says that our book is being reissued
But he doesn't seem to think we're very incidental to it.
Come over soon, people. Fly us out to Oakland
People play the fucking piano there & stuff
People are blue, people are violet, Camille Pissarro
Is leaning against the trash can, adjusting the brim
Of his hat, people might go blind & touch
The finely leather chair & let the basil leaf make a cup
On their fingertip. People won't be over for an hour
I'm not mad at anyone today, oh but I still hate them
Maybe this feeling of mine interferes with some of my friendships.
People must imitate others so they can go on
Even when they're old enough to be original quote unquote
People are a monkey in the living room of John Maynard Keynes

He is also a monkey there, I have a primitive headache.
People never wanted to sound bitter like on stage
They wanted life to feel sweet a flower tiny in the leaves
People adore their own vices, but they are skeptical of everyone else's
They will found the good society on their own vices I think.
Camille Pissarro would like a tube of white paint please.
He should get a job teaching art, he has no flash.
That guy doesn't have too many expensive items
Eeeh! one of them already fell off!
Oh god she *is* horrible; they came unexpectedly
One night. You should have shot her up. Painter's
Son Rapes Aunt. Hey Auntie! Just a small one, Dear
People talk disgusting & have fun. They watch
Baseball on TV and say get those bums out . . . This TV
Has sunstroke . . . Oh fuck fucking unintelligible
Pills are herbs. People join the navy & go to Tahiti
Am Here Books? Styx doesn't wanna outrage
The bourgeoisie any more. Die pretty. People are lames.
People are doing the homerun trot against background of some China.
People's orange zinnias have few leaves & stunted growth.
People are too tired to remember thing. People dream
They are fighting in the Civil War with their pal Rose.
People get shell-shocked & give talismans to friends
The amaryllis wilts, the Queen-Anne's-lace gets cobwebby
Heavy air, big orange moon, something sad
& inevitable happens to someone else, a little to you
People keep talking, modulate, safe conduct
She wouldn't marry someone who wasn't any fun
O Tamar, dance on my butter, the lady at the
Chinese store has a new hairdo – I said, "You have a new
Hairdo?" "Oh yes, cut it." I see no reason why not
People go for the woman's market lately

By good I don't mean, I mean that I mean memory
Of good feeling. It would be fun to see you anyway
People can always be around just about all evening. Sure
People can surprise & whomp out a good. People
Are born in a trunk. Bums (see previously.)
I'm just making lighthearted conversation to cheer you up.
I wish he were in town to consult on about six things
'Cause no one else is literate. Are we almost there? No.
I'll finish your juice. People wonder if politics doesn't
Mean others can lie now, people wonder if the
Transparency of the lie is supposed to be somehow
Beautiful, people have a headache between their eyes,
They are suddenly plural in their rows of chairs
They themselves are quiet, they go home & put their head under a blanket.
People don't sleep well but they don't mind
They like a little read, they like a little story.
People are appreciative of the virtue known as charm
Camille Pissarro is feeling a little down, a shadow hopeful
People's health will not be good for several more months
They are afraid they are leaving Cheyenne with regard to someone or thing
She is in her down phase, but isn't she just like Blind Raftery?
The sea is a waterbed the stars are a bedspread I'm
Afraid to sleep. People are having a personal romantic crisis
But the defense never rests, the sea wolves are my
Pals, & there's these Mediterranean fruitflies
Or some such things like that . . . "And Pharoah's little daughter . . ."
Have you got to the sad parts? Some people think like
That. Jesus it's only a quarter to twelve.

NEW YEAR'S EVES

Once, in Marrakech, no – Boys
turn your lights out now (I
can't remember) – Once, I
think, once Ron Padgett took me
to the theatre, in Marrakech, to
a performance, in French, of
THE BANGLADESH CONCERT. In
the stage version actors sang the
rock singers' songs & played
the music of Ravi Shankar, Ali
Akbar Khan, etc. The stage version
didn't work well in French, but
Ron loved it & so, so did I
especially the beautiful Moroccan
boy who played Bob Dylan –
too beautiful but with that Monroe-ish
glow that compensates for beauty too –
that was too long ago. Did Ron also
                kiss me?

One New Year's Eve, Ed Dorn
Jenny & Ted & I were in the small
back-yard of Chicago, with our
meth among the late lilacs & snow –
Ted had to go to New York & come
back, the same night, in Steve
Hamilton's Volvo, which he did
do, making one hundred
dollars in the reading he gave
at the Annual New Year's Eve

Reading at the Falling Star
Bookstore, Dress-shop, & Pavilions —
He arrived home with his fee
at 1:31 which we spent on
my pregnancy test & guacamole —
Most of us rested on New Year's Day, but
Jenny & I shot a movie
in which we dreamed America was a park
in London.

Once, in London, I got so tired on
New Year's Eve, Chip Delany cooked
the leg of lamb for me, & still I
got so tired I was just me
now in America no matter
what. And Chip said, So
what? If your friends are
heroes, then of course the
years aren't. America
is where the Block is but we don't
care so we just live there, because
that's where they get to have us,
us heroes of the non-book part
So Bless your heart & try to
get into the book too, if you
                    want to.

Once, I got into the wrong book
but I changed it. I did this
every year, by ignoring
my life. Since everyone else
ignored my life too,

no one knows what's happening
to them. Have I made it so
no one can know
about their life in its entirety?
                    No.
         But, Once,

on New Year's Eve, my father
poured me a glass of champagne
& said, "Now what, Lib?" And I said
"Perhaps this year I won't know
anyone." And he said, "That wouldn't
              be nice."

As You Like It

I'm so with it I can't believe it.
Well yeah some were but I have this folder I keep.
Certainly.
Hi. You going out today?
You tell Mommy buy you ice cream.
You tell Mommy go fuck self.
Hi.
Okay.
Tell Bobby to call me up some time, there's a girl who's gonna
kill herself if Allen doesn't come to her farm.
Okay.
Listen when she's hypnotizing you let your mind do whatever
it wants & it'll all happen by itself.
Okay honey, have fun. Bye bye.
Shelley's getting hypnotized.
If you love a rainy night you'll love tonight.
Can we go outside? it's still light time.
Doll?
Hi, how are you?
He don't bother us no more.
This is CBS FM in a white tux & tails
He's a good boy now?
We're not enemies no more.
These people that are nuts, they're mostly these
adolescents waiting for postcards. My sense of this one is
just to note it & let it go.
But I gave her a hug & a little squeeze.
We used to listen to La Boheme a lot.
It's very funny, they're unbelievable Bohemians, they
cough a lot.

Just like the days of old into the mystic.

*

How could a meteorite grow?
This April grey is green.
That girl who pretends she's a Martian is really right. See
she's right. She's always right.
Pine-scented rosemarinus
Let's call up George & ask him if we can have 6 vases
because our morale is low.
Say hello to the knife I killed your father with.
Hi knife.
What did you do with the royal bracelet?
Watch out the killers are here!
You like this movie? God no one will even talk.
Today because of the space monster, it is a dead world.
Spinoza liked plants. And fountains.
Well this is quite a surprise. You didn't go home after all.
We stayed with the Prophetess.
The Prophetess has quite a bosom.
You are in a deep sleep. But your brain is awake isn't it?
Who are you really?
I am a Martian.
Thousands are looting a liquor store near Johannesburg.
Present temperature 60 degrees.
I'm gonna go outside now.
It's raining, honey.
How do you know?
I can hear that the street is wet. Wait! See? It's
raining on the fire escape.
Gloria Steinem will speak at length on abortion.

Can I have 35¢ for baseball cards?
I just want to be in my life!
Where are you?
In my life!
I am a black lace fan.
I need the paper & the many little mineral waters.
Unacceptable to Winfield & Jackson.

*

I saw 2 sweet lesbians kissing in the rain, they were
probably mourning the death of Mozart.
That's exactly what they were doing.
I want to read Paul Taylor's memoirs. They all say things
like, Then me & Jasper fucked. That's a lie.
This is a terrific article.
God I'm so wet.
How the hell will poets ever get to see anything if everybody
knows what we look like?
Look at that, it says God Castigated the Ostriches for
Their Stupidity. When did he do that? I must not have
been there.
Hello is this Bobby?
You prick.
Her imaginative inventions are sort of not as good as her
I love you poems.
Tom Carey's gonna become a little pen pal.
With the German gay guy.
Okay Bob.
Hi.
Raining out right?
If I was a policeman I'd arrest Grace immediately.

So what's your hubby doing tonight?
You guys are in your rooms doing It?
Yeah that's what they're gonna do.
Yeah the couch fell on his head.
How can you tell if it's sexist or just its story is? It's
like saying This bottle will make you drunk.

*

My husband is in your building having a tooth extracted
by Dr. Berger the famous pimp.

*

He stupidly entered the elephant's trunk.
A man is singing in the quandary near the liquor store.
A quartz brain ravaged my friend as he lay abed last night
while Valium eluded him.
Who is this cat?
Her name is Doll.
My lifespan is elastic but I am sad with spangles of & upon me.
I am just a little pot of coffee.
Ah God Oh Honey sore sweet love squi . . .
But it was kind of nice aside from the realities of it all.
There's snow on my necklace.
What was it like?
It was real life there, it was still comedy but just a
notch higher a little just a little bit too closer to tragedy.

*

Would you make me something?
No I'm tired.
Please, you don't mind, I'm starving but my mouth is still

sore. There's 3 strawberries cut them up into little pieces
& put lots of sugar & milk on them.
I dreamed you were with 2 detectives, they looked like
Frank Sinatra & that other guy in *High Society*. And you
were like on Noah's Ark protecting all the animals & the
children. Except it was your mother's house in a town
like a suburb in Kansas.
My idea of going to the dentist is that it hurts to go
there even just to hold the real patient's hand.
Did she really say that?
Yeah. Pretty good huh?
That was when he didn't understand she was just a girl on
pills being charming. But he unfortunately thinks that's
life. And so they go on.
Here's the part about leading the turkey on the leash.
Here's the part about going down to the beach to shoot
some clams.

*

You don't change your drug habits though you might change
your attitude.
That's what I've been trying to tell you.
He said the press said he always struck at the first pitch
& he knew it was true. Then why'd he do it this guy asked.
Because it made him feel so good, he said & then he beamed.
Carmine said he never heard of housemaid's knee.
That's very funny.
Girls came in asking for fake fingernails & he & the assistant
guy were looking all over for fake fingernails. One bleached
punk tall girl said Those drawers where you keep the fake
fingernails have been here since 1886.

Come back! We found the fingernails.

Now I have to decide what color fingernails I want.

I just made up a great aphorism, you want to hear it? It says,
'There's nothing funnier than things that are funny.' I
don't think it'll go.

I'm reading this book 3 BRICKS SHORT OF A LOAD.

I had a fantasy in the kitchen someone said to me, "How
come you do everything & write your works out of feeling
not out of reason?" And I said, "It doesn't feel right the
other way."

After publishing her once.

Maureen said no because she thought she had integrity.

Are you his girlfriend?

That's something I've been meaning to ask him.

My apothecary is named Carmen, she is beautiful & she sweetens
my imagination.

That's the only people I'm publishing.

★

She came in like a girl bursting out of a cake & said
"I didn't do anything bad at the bar."

Were you drunk?

God was I.

I've got to get up so my daughter can lead me 30 miles closer
to Colonus. I learned two things from the play last night,
God is Love, & When you're dead you're dead.

Look at this picture, that was his look that when
he looked at you like that you felt terrific.

I'll never get to meet him.

I'll never get to see him again.

What's it like out?

The way it's supposed to be this time of year, it's warm
& people feel erotic. George is painting cunnilingus on a
vase, & Bernadette's translating dirty Greek epigrams. She's
playing Sarah Vaughn, he's playing Brahms.

*

This is a tale inside your tale. You sat down & wrote this.
You are on Holy Ground.
How do I propitiate them?
Heaven is like being in the middle of writing this poem &
it's only itself, heaven.
A cup & wine, they'll tell you.
I can't buy *my* voice telling me about *my* poem.
It's almost the time.
Everything I say here is true because I see it, when
I'm here.
I'm going to be the tutelary deity of here. That's one part.
Devotion. This is something you have to know. You
don't stand for it, you demand it. Of yourself & them.
Then you can rest in the arms of the god & they can suffer
& suffer like you did & then. You gave them love. Your
end is sweet. All this woe was love because you were
together. You give your body to the place is very im-
portant too.
All those anecdotes are about how somebody was good somewhere.
It's time to make dinner.
You don't even get a cup of coffee for intention.

*

Feed the cat Ted.
Kill yourself.

Nah.

There's a woman in it.

Part of this dirty song I used to know.

I'm liking it so far.

If you would participate one evening.

I'm gonna be there in June.

How one . . . I'm going to make a circle around me. I'm
going to go back just far enough, I'm going to tell the
climate like it was for me,

Whose town is San Francisco? Whose town is New York?

*

I just wrote on these 2 big linoleum prints & now I feel
nuts. 'Cuz first of all it's no fun to be an artist, your
wrist falls asleep & things like that.

& then on the flowerpot it says flower.

I said I can't find anyplace to write bush.

He brambled all night long, till a preacher cut him down.

I want an artist to come over & fix it.

A stepladder with an ear in it.

It's from this series called "Desert Visions."

What's Uncle Lewie doing?

With all the little pickaninnies bringing us yogurt.

This guy was great he was my hero on 13th Street just
past Third Avenue.

Farout guys. It was very beautiful actually.

Nothing, which is about what he knows.

I'm glad I'm not going to be responsible for hurting you
anymore, because I'm in love with you.

What're you gonna do tonight?

I am a poor wayfaring fuckup.

I told him she said he doesn't go around having any thoughts
like that, what does he think about I said, he just goes
around giggling, she said, he's a poet.
Well I hope I get up early tomorrow & type.
Last night I dreamed I was on the road forever with Allan
& Phyllis.
What's a desert girl like me doing in socks?
He dislocated his finger in his sleep last night. He
decided to get George to set it, everyone told him Katie
has lots of tongue depressors you can use for splints.
Him, Guy Pène du Bois said he didn't drink enough, so
he says I have since remedied this.
Beauty Beauty Beauty
He was in love with me in 1865.

*

Everybody's soft on Eileen.

*

Maybe it's just paranoia, all rich people get it.
Grey with green clouds of leaves, & I was
breathless waiting for April etc. so I . . .
Who took the tacks?
You have filthy hands.
I'm a witness to that.
Señor I am very poor, it is Easter & the children have no
money for chocolate bunnies.
That duck took our money.
I am that duck
Fuck.
What are you doing?

What do you think?
I'm Bob Kerr in Washington.
Lookit how pretty the eggs come out.

★

He has come from another form of love.
He is a great beauty with humane eyes.
He is in the middle of the Fourth.
She took on the Toronto Bluejays for a lark. All right Bill.
Easter means you won't be lonesome any more because your
baby brother bear got born.
He said his life was already so long because of all the miles
he's travelled, 44,000.
Then they moved on to Cleveland.
He says one of my wives is from Mars & one is ga-ga.
Then she said I married you & I didn't even get a green card.
I'm reading Othello.
That's very funny.
I'm thinking about how various people would say that. Ted
would call up & say I'm lying here drinking this pepsi &
talking to the boys & reading Othello. I would say, I
seem to be reading Othello. Googoo would say, I've been
reading Othello & it's uh very interesting.
What did I say?
You said, I'm reading Othello.
Lookit, our favorite movie.
What is it?
El Condor.
That guy's awful. Awful people are all right.
Hi, I'm from New England, I'm having a weird day.
The Bluejays nothing.

★

You might want to talk about it in terms of its difference.
It would be an act of generosity.
Generosity killed the cat.
But getting around the periphery of some similar kind of
thing. As I was moved toward trying it by these & by who I
am not. I don't want there to be any secrets tòld.
Instead how my shoulder feels when I turn this corner of
the left or whatever, finally to say that.
Pretty lavender plant, help me to make a go of it.
Me too.
Me too.
Right.
You can't pay me because you can't afford me, ever.
You may go down to Hades, I may stay on earth, but they can't
ever have either of us.
I am my own French translation.
So?
I want to be person in time, rather than personality.
It was not suitable for a newspaper. It was subjective in a
formal way.
It was fantastic.
Don't be dumb now.
Allen said Exactly. Tell them *why* you have a stomach-ache.
Has this funny thing going of this girl & it just goes on like
a quest a few bumps bruises & pains are the least of her
worries.
I do love the down on his cheek though.
She does catch that person herself quite well.
How can she get through anything without something truly
awful happening?
This quest don't say beauty.

So I said loving the idea still of the glamor of funny
& guilt & being alive.
Because she wants to amuse you turn you on & enhance your
journey.
Behind the screen she beats you with her fists when you need it.
Now the reason I coughed there was to facilitate thee so
& so on.

*

Right after Easter Antigone left for Thebes.
Her father & brother got the golden rest.
She's still having her morning coffee.
She don't want to talk to Anselm Edmund or the wall yet.
Steve said *Antigone* would make her unbearable.
My mother's sending us a dirty joke in the mail.
Sas-quatch.
He's on the rag now because he took too many pinkies.
It was about, something about, you know, got anything in
the icebox?
Well what do you think?
Actually I have to go home.
So I should give *you* some money?
Well that would be terrific if you could.
Fuck you & your sick kid too, you say & then he yawns.
He's not that part that wants to be asleep.
You're really very blithe.
All day hove to in the lough.
Anyone knows about anything.
She can not yield to trouble nor could he.
It was an elaborate exercise in sophistry as to whether or
not a crime was committed.

There are so many of these attitudes around right now as to
what's true that you can understand it as a rule that the
opposite of the prevailing attitude is true.
But then, what? Poor cactus.
Poor me.
Do you ever use an object?
In fucking?
The Blessed Ones have caused my face to begin to get wrinkled.
Oh horse dick that's what I say.
Have I asked the fucking cosmos to treat me like horsedicks
or what?

*

You know how your arm looks far away when you're lying
in bed?
Do you ever go around seeing your nose?
Dick Mock had an affair with a ninety-year-old from my
home town.
He has a foot in both worlds.
I saw one of them.
The gift comes down and I'm sweating like a pig.
This is a postcard of a world-famous sign.
This is a beauty all by itself.
LAVENDER SPIKE.
My heart yearns for that 5 o'clock in the morning feeling.
His exile & awesome end.
He is the brokedown cadillac of divine justic, speaking a
fusile tongue:
Die, motherfucker.
There's too much electricity in the kitchen. All the way
in the living room it's making the asparagus fern break out

into tiny white blossoms.
He says like, Are you going to this big art blowout tonight?
the one that's in the basement of Sun Lee's Hardware Store.
My poem just stopped being about Colonus again.
I feel fucked over in a not unpleasant way.
I used to have this duck whose head was on wrong. He would
run around in circles with one eye always looking up.
I used to get high on mescaline & go over to the park & paint
names on the trees like George & Lydia.

*

This is the tale at the end of.
No it isn't.
Hey I put the ending in the middle.
You are still on Holy Ground.
Nothing special happening.
I can't seem to end it 'cause it's my life when did it start?
I bet you're tired.
Not really.
Mom wanna see Tarzan?
Look he's missing a leg 'cause it's under a hill.
Gamble on the run at right.
Oh boy, the old time catches
'Cause I'm gonna clean the game & I don't want it to get dirty.
A wasting away to knowledge.
Guess what I'm making now?
Power Droid.
Editor's note: Ha Ha.
I'm looking for my blue & I can't find it.
Where's the scissors?
Ouch you're on my toe.

He got his kidney stone to get into my journal.
Actually I'm completely discreet.
I've always prided myself on saying the worst thing at the
least appropriate time.
Who's your favorite singer?
My favorite singer is Eddie.
Nah. Buddy Holly?
Me.
Elvis Presley?
Me.
Bob Dylan?
Me.
Buckets of rain, buckets of tears, buckets of bumblebees
stuck in my ears.
It's so easy to fall in love.
Boogie Boogie Boogie.

Dark Thought

"you cannot discourage your wingspread"

POSTCARDS

Feb. 17

Dear Barney,
 The ashtray is full & the
natives are listless, but
there is a swell love hang-
ing out on the corner where
they sell souvenirs to the
grenadiers & girls from the
seaside. I have bought me
a pink culotte & a racy
sort of vest to wear with
those remarkable earrings
you gave me. How are
you & that boy who's a
man whom you did
that to on the day after
Valentine's Day? The
weather here is good for
taking the wrinkles out
of clothes (rainy)
                  Love,
                      May

                    *

Feb. 18

Dear Reginald,
     I still love your body
most aberrantly being con-
sumed with hatred of your
loathesome soul which
refuses to lend me your
body for a single violet
evening of your stay at
our picturesque little
resort which is all that
we have here except for
too briefly you—I keep
your lost or castoff cig-
arette holder the ivory one
with me always but
you are mean, mean,
mean! Jesus & Buddha
are made nervous &
sad by your cruelty to
humanity, me—
                    Love,
                         Congetta

                    *

Feb. 19

Dear Fuckface,
    Everyone thinks you're
the Goddess of Compassion
but I know you also have
piles & a scarcely controlled
urge to sing for a living.
So much for you. Here
everything is stupid as I
have a dwindling flu
which necessitates my
finally paying attention to
my dwindling pocketbook.
How about some bucks,
Goddess Baby? any amount
above five I'd appreciate &
continue to light at your
altar the incense I steal
from the neo-Rocky Mountain
healthfood store. I
still like you either way,
                Love,
                    Bubbles

                    *

Feb. 25

Dear Nutso,
    Wal, it's pretty blank
around here. The cat
is hungry, & Hubby hasta
get up early (those two
paired are not a sig-
nificance for your cheap
little mindlessness to ponder).
How could I ever
miss you? everytime I
do I slap myself on my
cheek & read a chapter of
The New Hairdresser's Manual.
If you should
ever get normally sentient
enough to notice the
weather, you might drop
a line to your,
            XXX
              Margie

*

March 6

Dear Francis,
    I miss you very much
although you are always
here too—there I go, in
trouble in a sentence, dis-
tracted by the weather, so
silky-aired like Hawaii,
which (weather) is reminding me
of you while I am being
distracted from you,
from writing to you. I
guess you *are* the weather
practically, & today I
like the weather so much;
& also I can be *in it*
without thinking, & on
rainy days blame you
for acting like I have to
grow up, like a hollyhock
or something, so I'm
going for a walk—
                        Alice

APRIL

What if he doesn't like me
how will he find me there where I am
how will he find the same me
that I am? What if

getting older means that
no one ever finds you, there
where you are, where they see you?
What if they get older

the same way a different way?
What if he won't let himself be found?
I know I'll like him, I'd
look for him, but what if

he can't find me? while
I'm there? like some others can't?

2/26/83 FOR TENNESSEE WILLIAMS

I dedicate this bath to him
this self-serving bath
in herbed water a
thin blue towel to
swath wet hair—
I'm so hungover

You defended Kowalski
& I defended Blanche
for 3 hours in Buffalo
July of 1970—I'm
mad at you still
for being as right as
I was so passionately
myself—how I loved how
I felt!

There will be
mothers & sisters to
accompany one through
the underwater tunnel
to a foliate loss of being
yellow rose & anemone
purple: the house
bouquet

All those movies that
shaped my face—did
he hate their not being
the plays? but it

comes through, the poetry
a whole transparent
animal, so "not repulsive"
a wonder of us. You'll see if
you look at my face—
(Oh how I still like it!)

Then what man would be in the
tunnel with them? with him? it

must be the brother
self who is always
dead & is perfectly
beautiful: A Hellenic

Mycenaean name of
him? No, older.
Younger. No name
but that one I now say:

the forever one.

Song Book

to everybody.
Why don't you think of a solution
to my problems that's amenable
to me? You can't. You're all
failures. So I have to do it
myself & make you disbelieve
my truth. I'm tired of this

poem. I don't want you to give me
everything I want you to help
me think better. That's a lie. I
don't want to think. I don't want
to be given things. I want to be
given. Anyone can give me.
Give me. Give

you. It's bad to love tightly. You
could give me to you if I didn't
have to be you to suit your desires.
You want to give you to you—
that's a platitude I heard in a
truth book that everyone read.
I don't believe it but do I
love you? It's not that I try
but that I find myself
caught in an air with you without
my picture

anyone anywhere love, but we don't
have hardly anything to eat

except of self, strange hot fall
don't eat me dears I'm doing
that well myself, not
being given. Leave me alone
don't leave me alone

to whom am I speaking to? blue,
blue wings. (No faces.) Don't tell me a thing.

Bob & Simon's Waltz

"People never seem to change at all—only their
children do. Last time I was in Buffalo there was
Sabina & there was this baby, & now Sabina's grown
so tall, & Alice is Sabina."

                            Tom Raworth

                ★

"You had fun with your friend, Dick."
"I still haven't figured out if he's queer yet. He's
the most ordinary person I've ever met."
"What about me?"
"Don't flatter yourself."

                        Alice Notley
                        Ted Berrigan
                        Doug Oliver

                ★

"Joanne . . . How was she? I only spent time with her
once; she & I & Anselm Hollo went walking on the
beach at 4 o'clock in the morning."

                            Tom Raworth

                ★

"When I'm with him I feel like I'm with this complete
social outcast. He says all he does is have fights

at home & go out & get drunk."

Eileen Myles

*

"I had this dream . . . I guess. Well it must've been you
& then your sister came in . . . interesting positions . . .
then it turned into this Maurice Girodias book . . . & I
could see the page numbers & everything – so I decided
it must be time to wake up."

Ted Berrigan

*

"Don't ever leave here, Alice, unless there's a really
good reason."

Tom Raworth

*

"Does she want her envelope stuffed or creased?"

Alice Notley

*

"You're so beautiful, that I'm saying goodbye."

John Daley

*

"You married a guy because he was alive."

Ted Berrigan

★

"She . . . gets paler . . . in the evening."

Doug Oliver's Scottish aunt, Mamie

★

". . . I guess I don't know what I'm asking, exactly . . .
maybe I'm just projecting."
"In that case, Yes."

Bob Rosenthal
Doug Oliver

★

"She's walking off into the mist."
"She's got a great walk when she's walking off into the mist."

Bob Rosenthal
Doug Oliver

★

"I'd like to write these poems in which I say right out,
'I'm really very naive.'"

Doug Oliver

★

"Are you saying you've outgrown Dylan Thomas?"
"No. I'm not saying I've outgrown Dylan Thomas. I'm
saying I read him a lot when I was sixteen or seventeen
years old."
"It would be terrible if people outgrew a great poet like
Dylan Thomas."
"Yes, it would be."
"People don't outgrow great poets . . . people don't outgrow
Yeats."
"You don't outgrow your life."

Doug Oliver
Woman at poetry reading

★

"I heard you were humiliated because you thought Mercedes
McCambridge was a man & found out she wasn't."
"Well, yes, frankly I was."

Alice Notley
Doug Oliver

★

"You have the wrong thing in your hand."

Alice Notley

★

"I had a long talk with Bob about your finances."

Doug Oliver

★

"Do you ever think about technique?"

Doug Oliver

*

"I brought you some flowers."
"I need some."

Wendy Mulford
Alice Notley

*

"You gave him a very sweet look when you kissed him goodbye last night."

Ted Berrigan

*

"My angel Doug has gone away; & my sweetheart Tom Pickard; & my new girlfriends, Denise & Wendy."

Ted Berrigan

*

"Does Marion still have that willowy figure?"

Doug Oliver

*

"I remember this time at Gordon's, when Jan was across
the room, & she was plotzed but she gave me this pur-
poseful look, & walked across the room, but she was
plotzed, but she decided to walk as if purposefully gliding . . .
And then she came & sat down beside me. And then she kissed
me on the cheek. Just as if she were Joanne & I was
Ebbe & had just said something dumb . . . as if she were saying
Oh Ted."

Ted Berrigan

Alice Notley
May 9, 1982

At the End-of-School Party

You have our old cat? She is a very beautiful cat. She is
very smart. We have her since she is two weeks old, we feed
her a little milk and butter. Once she catch a . . . you know those
animals in the house? She catch it with her claws. My
husband teach her not to put out her claws so when she catch
this . . . I can't remember the name of this little animal . . . she
show my husband her claws first and ask him if it's okay.
My husband also teach her to open up the envelope of cat food.
And the boys are playing with her all the time. But my
husband is sick . . . he have to have an operation, a colostomy.
There is so much medicine, and this bag . . .and the cat scratch
the bag. I tell *them* this, I say the cat scratch up the
furniture too much so we can't keep her. But, no, we like
her very much. It is because of this, this bag. So when
your son says your cat runs away and you need a new cat, I
send her over right away. My husband is very sick . . . What's
wrong? I don't know. He has seven doctors, and they all say
a different thing. There are two doctors at Mount Sinai
Hospital, and two doctors at Manhattan Hospital, and two
doctors at Roosevelt Hospital, and another one . . . But my son
Johnny and your youngest son are taking care of this black
cat with white . . . have you seen it? You haven't seen it?
I'm sure it is sick. It was in our doorway in a box, and
it didn't move for two days. Two days! It has a terrible
smell. I'm sure it is sick. They see it and they come
back and say, It still hasn't moved. Our old cat has two
names, the Portuguese name and Doll. Yes. But when the
boys see her one time at our house, they come home and say
to me, She doesn't know me any more.

HOMAGE TO MARIANNE MOORE

I can go there almost anytime
some days take a while
it's a picture
of a cascade of a pattern
a woman sleeps in that sleeve
Charlie McGrath smiles at me
I get mad there too
I guess that that's how I know it's
heaven, my home . . .

. . . Now I have to improve this
poem by making it longer & a
mess. Useless to the massive
brain. She's gotta fall off her toes
you made. "I didn't know you
were writing." "I wasn't. I
was breaking."
There's this
very interesting man. He lives in
this building. He gets up every
morning, & he goes outside & is
this man. He wears a man jacket
& a man hat & a good-day smile
'cause he's this man. He dresses
off-decade but he talks good, he's
had two heart attacks & he's still
there, very. He's this man. He makes
my life heaven, though I barely
know him I know heaven. I know
that I believe I'm engaged in
discourse with my friend. I suspect

she hates me. Does she make
my life heaven? "And the anger
that was the birds making sounds
at each other, was music to some
harmless to most, who knows
what a bird feels? Not even,
maybe, a bird does when it's talking"
And so I

In heaven you watch a lot
of television. Side-effects of heaven
cause the dreams of See in
heaven & there's all this sorrow so
the sun in Jerusalem can't be
"in" it so there's all this sorrow
like a compartment that floods
the lower berth so your hero
you got to chair the Pullman
roomette with I mean share
see the point is that sorrow
having the ring of beauty to it
gives that ring to the hand of
marriage, I mean Heaven, here
on heaven, & sorrow is sung
& songs are from shock, of
shock though I honestly
& I no don't think I ever
expected anything to be
different than, than it is that's
how it's heaven & heaven isn't
satisfactory, that's really what
you mean. No it isn't. Satisfactory. It's Heaven.

Put You to Shame

Being sad you don't

have to be

serious—

Said the pompous

girl or boy to someone

you know—But

Everyone already

knew that; they

let her or him say that,

who then switched to sunlight, and

the victim improved too.

They didn't know we

were reading their

novel. Yes they did.

That's how they were

comforted by

knowing how to act.

And the thing about novels,

aren't the characters

better than

the readers?
I'm sorry I'm so
fascinated, you're tired
from working your own great role
so hard. But
tomorrow, we can
be on the
same side (no comfort
there). But what we are,
we're all friends, sometime
lovers, relatives, enemies.
We're bigger than the
cosmos, bigger than
religion. That's no
help either. Not even
something. It's
practically exhilarating,
boys & girls
together forever
till it's over,
how sad – no –
Edmund was

right, Ted, God

isn't Breath God's

Earth. So that

when you "go down" –

well you get

what I mean, that

Old Grandma

(right!) met

God, just a little

more intimately.

Breath is life, but

God isn't Breath –

God is gross: & that's why

we put up with Her.

In our novel

she must, perforce,

be as good as us.

DEAR MRS. BERRIGAN

—When I'm
slipping I
say, Hey
this is
okay!

           —It's when
           I'm standing
           upright that I
           feel worried—
           I feel stiff.

★

Pilot
Dark
Vida
Blue.

★

My thyme plant
looks like
frozen
combed
hair.

★

Mother & Brother Son

—Covered thou must
dance thee here, ship
by mark of land
or star.

59

★

What Does She
Keep In That Drawer?

gold dust
talcum
love dust
dirty sock dust
cubic dust
blank dust
blent dust
past dust

tin-past-tin
Summer, nineteen something-eight

★

I have been in-
tending to send you
money before but
I keep forgetting.
Love,
Mom

★

SUN

face of big gold woman, old

doesn't
have to smile 'cause
is already the Sun.

★

"for Geo. Schneeman"

"Study (for
'Stunning
Vase w/hole
in it')"
#237

★

Some call it ship,
Some call it face.

★

Phil's Wife

"You don't even know
you're listening, do you?"

★

BAD ANYTHING

Too much clear,
Not enough obscure.

It is never too late to start a new
way of thinking

:Said the pink flamingo to
the beavertail cactus.

★

"Here's the famous poet
& here's his former subject matter."

         ★

No
these
I'm
tell me
the sense
George & Ted
it says virtue
an early Greek, but
no, the body goes
by habit. In the
'love is leading us to
find out.'

         ★

May 15

". . . we're keeping
   our fragility
      to ourselves . . ."

         ★

song,

    for your air,

               love,

         ★

Love & Kisses,

The Death of Montcalm

★

PARTS OF THE BODY

face
shoe
chair
nose
boat

★

BAD NIGHT

as I fall
 asleep I
  might become
   her—

  (you don't
   get it.)

★

Top of the hour

each thing that
each thing
is its dream journal

★

A

fish dying

& it's raining

(blood)

★

Rice
&
Sardines

★

I can't re-
member if it's a
dream or a
story.

★

"what's an old
map like that
doing in a new
Indian like
this?"

★

Dear Mrs. Berrigan:

64

CONGRATULATING WEDGE

All things belie me, I think, but I
look at them though. Well boys, at
least you're not dead, right? What's
the date today? Until something. What?
Of the lady of the whitening blow.
I'm ashamed to keep on babbling
as if I've always been oneself,
diamond flow through. Humble
flannel skeleton. Grin, laugh unbecoming
Living at the bottom of the water may
have been obvious all the time. But
I forget. What's my plot? Hand
of a child, paw of an animal. Paint
it red & make a paw-print in the psalter.
Protect her & give her back her hat
Entangle her dreams in demotic and
Warm her feet; cheat the judge
& protect the tree from which he was carved.

*

And now that I've explained the situation
Jesus my frame hurts, you say.
Fucking pain. Hey come & empty my ashtray
once more & don't get so excited. A
gentle heart was broken. Whose? No one's
It's a figure like a frame among
medlars & briars. Hand me that piece of
that, just that, yeah. I don't mean it,
I've never meant anything because that's
not what I do, in the mountains I call home
How can I tell you of my wound? it's
round & silver & headstrong, it's
nothing more than temperament born
of a custom involving a circuitous journey
This is all wrong. It rains today, my
son's singing love songs of this
country, already being ten.

*

And if to withstand this nocturnal pollution of the tiny
wanton stars with bent hook clauses of misprision
I'm supposed to sing the melody of an unexpecting part . . .
Hey a pretty honey come a listen to me
while I evening, darling, your messages,
what would you think then? But I
wouldn't do that. Light surrounded oranges
towels clouds. You don't think you're my you.
Not here not you. You still think you're he. she.
Because I wouldn't "you" you, would I? I only
"you" some other he. she. I
who write poems. When she writes them,
it's different . . . A world of words, right?
It's only my version of *The Entertainer*
Nothing truly personal, I'm way above that.
I've learned about it for a lot of days. I've
been to see the doctor & you have to have shots
for it. 17 balls of yarn & a sewing machine.

★

No I wouldn't know why anyone would
want to write like that. I should never
have had to do it. We were used to this
other thing we always know like when we're
here. And you have this clear head & you're
seeing things & there they are. You don't
notice they're spelled. That's how you
know you're alive. I never saw you
looking like a dictionary definition & if I
did I wouldn't tell *nobody.* People
aren't like that. They say, Hey
asshole motherfucker turn that radio
off! *But the sun's playing on it!* But
it ain't real, you dumb package!
I recognize every package the way it
comes. Now I'm mixed up. But I
always wanted to be a package, person
thinks. Do they? Or, I gotta de-
fine this package, me. Or, God if only
I was a package but I'm not.

★

Walking backwards makes me cry, tiny
roses die. Oooh! I would like to prove
not only that do I? I do not, have a mind, but
I am vigorous. Instead you want some
instructions. Okay, and this is serious:
take good care of your skin. It's like
leather; wash it, oil it. Especially
watch your neck—even at your age,
in the city, your neck is dirty a lot. Taking
good care of your skin is like
sweeping the floor, no worse no
better. Some of these monks should learn it.
Not just vitamins & diet either. You have to
rub stuff on you all over yourself.
It's part of a philosophy I won't
go into yet, 'cause I gotta get
back to my other kind of talking or the
vessel will sink. I mean, you
gotta brush your hair, too
toss it & play with it too. Everything
must be cared for. The problem of
America is my body.

*

How can you love me & keep on singing?
You have to be saying something else, and
Hey light years don't (scratched) (torn)
        illeg.
windowbox.

            Not on a star loom so tired
territory braid's all frazzled, chairs among
the branches of my little fatigue trees
hold up violet amber crystal kids, mine
The only spinning vacancy is I, where I'm
going. The outright mystery of . . . I
forget. Here's a photo of the actual path
of least resistance. Sun shine on
broke mass. We will be intense tomorrow
when the omens are vivacious like . . . ?

                    ★

Polemic divine. I was insensibly led into it
that room. Together, touch, at high speed
until the molesters were killed. Then we
were free ship, whistling & swimming and being
our own furnish a place to hide. Take on a
smoky look on rock wall or tie of spider silk
It's all a look? Which bright with orange
The first thirty pages are a little wet.
I'll never get in any human interest again
because I'm no longer a dolphin.
It's so lovely out I'm nostalgic for
Indiana & the Inn there. Some-
where in room where face-dancing I had to
say something stupid in order to live,
like . . . I can't think right now
of anything stupid to say.

★

She ceaselessly changes for thine such chains as these
name of your country & why you are in chains
the gift I have made for you, my love & praise or
       blame I must receive
playful waters into tawny feathers
love affair to light breeze —
the smallest constituents of matter are
tiny tiny snowflake affairs each different from
       every other
they're always changing, each, but why? for
       their own amusement . . .
Hey Daddy, after this should I put on some country?
grief, were musical from place to place
I found aspirin & change for Mommy. One
penny. When my senses were restored I
was all the lines to the song "Blue Skies"
& my older son was singing me incessantly
Even though I was a song I still washed
all his shirts & made his dinner
Later I was freed to become "Blue Eyes
       Crying in the Rain"
& Later was finally freed to become
The cat jumped down & grabbed my foot!

May–June 1983

Margaret and Dusty

Margaret wrote a letter
sealed it with her finger
put it in her pocket
for the Dusty Baker

Dusty was his bat
Dusty was his moustache
Dusty was Margaret's pocket
They both got all dusty

If I had a flower
If I had a trinket of gold
      & silver & lapis
If I had a medal & a trophy
      & a fullup sticker album
I'd rather be all dusty
Like those two friends of mine.

Sweetheart

If I address it to you I have not, have I,
let go of you yet. I'm sorry.

"Goodnight, Mom."   "Goodnight, Honey."

And before that I saw a white leopard
leap across my room. I'm
not wearing contacts, have flu

It's been quite a day. Shaky
Snow is white
I would like not to think, it
makes me foreigner of myself I'd like

this strange enrichment of the
spirit I feel though bereft
but I'd like this lovely inadequate
apartment
but I'd like my music
my mental music not to
suddenly render me rawly sad
"You have empty honey"   "Yes, I have"

this person who sleeps in my bed
she's slept there forever and yet
there was another
when it was another
bed looking so same so recently
but that I would have to remember
(strangely an involuntary measure)

O Poem really addressed
to me, it's you are found indulgent
fit and of comfort, lustre, real light
I praise you, thank you
for being what I have tonight

1/18/84

Design by David Duer. Type composition in Plantin by Annie Graham. Printed at McNaughton & Gunn. The use of acid-free paper and sewn signatures assures the reader of a long-lasting book.